AF656919

Mirrored Monologues

Finding Joy Through Introspection

notionpress.com

Mirrored Monologues

Finding Joy Through Introspection

Neena Kamal

notionpress.com

Notion Press

Old No. 38, New No. 6

McNichols Road, Chetpet

Chennai - 600 031

First Published by Notion Press 2015

ISBN 978-93-5206-564-6

Who looks outside dreams...

...who looks inside awakens!

Carl Jung

Contents

ACKNOWLEDGEMENTS

I knew her…
from somewhere…
I thought…

The look, the smile
The walk, the style
It was so much I know…
Difficult to place though…

I raised my hand, she raised it too,
Gesture superficial from both the sides though…
Hundred times I searched for the name…
Some relation to relate…
Shadow of my questions on her face too,
Gesture superficial from both the sides though…

Then I knew who she was,
My own reflection and mirror on the wall
For sure it was M!
Mirror was the culprit, made me feel…
It's some other world and it's not ME…

Was it the mirror or

Really a different world … a different ME…

So Unknown…

Even to me!

Neena, 2005

This book is a story of my journey to get closer to myself, and to accept my own choices and their respective consequences. There have been so many people who have helped me on this journey.

First of all, my father, who taught me the biggest lesson of my life: to accept the inevitable end of all our stories! But more on that later, in the book. My mother has been the constant factor in my pursuit of betterment. She ensures that I don't stagnate. My sister has been my companion to a certain extent on this path and I share a lot of learning with her.

I really feel blessed to be surrounded by so many friends and supporters who don't get surprised by my any new idea or adventure I embark upon. They are my strength!

I can just go on with a long list but there two people I should call my co-authors actually: Kamal, my better half in every sense of the term, my first reader and critic. If I really become a published author, I owe it to him totally! The other is Mona: I can't thank her enough, for she believed in this idea even before anybody else did! She was my partner in figuring out these concepts. She helped me with a lot of clarity which on my own I would not have achieved. Thanks Mona!

I thank all of them for being there for me always, and in all ways thinkable!

Finally, when I offer to share this journey with you, my readers, my heart is filled with gratitude to just reach your level of attention. I sincerely hope that you enjoy this journey as much as I have enjoyed it.

God, please bless whatever is true and worth!

INTRODUCTION

"Human being!" I just love these words. The person who invented this name might have looked at differently. But for me, it means that you are neither just human nor just being but you're being human and that's why you are a human being! There are so many aspects of being human. You can be compassionate, kind, loving, caring, understanding, giving, and when you have all these aspects and many more, you are being human and that's why you are called a human being!

I have spent 15 years in the corporate world, in a profession which very has conveniently replaced this word 'being' with something called 'resource.' Human resource. The moment the human becomes a resource he needs to be resourceful, productive, competent, profitable, and efficient! All these things are quite different from being human! In this case, the stress is on being a resource. This works wonders for the corporate sector. The skills we learn are also aligned with being the resource. We are educated and trained for such skills.

But what happens to the skills required to be a good human being? How much education or practice is spent on those? How do I know that I should be compassionate? Where do I learn to be kind? Can I be kind at my workplace? Or is the priority about being focused? There is absolutely no harm in being a good human resource. But what are we doing to the human being inside us? Does he or she get a breather? Or we are suffocating our human being selves?

In the process of being a good human resource, somewhere, each of us forgets the fun of being human, the fun of being the human being! Then, sometime in our lives, we get a reality check and try and wash all our sins away. That reality check is most often than not, very rude. It shows us how unhappy this façade is. It shows us a gap between the life we chose and the life we dreamt of. It shows how deep we are stuck in this struggle.

I got my reality check in a very crude way. I lost my father in a 20 minutes timeframe to a cardiac arrest. It shook me so deeply that I went through a phase of doubts and uncertainty.

Planning and organising were considered my strongest skills when I worked with the big MNCs. My bosses used to depend on robust plans I created and the way I implemented them. In my mind, I had no doubt that planning was the most essential thing in life. However, what I had forgotten to look at was that life has its own plans. I realised it when I lost my father. I realised that all the plans which I had for myself which included him were no longer relevant the day he left this world. In that grieving period for my father one of the biggest things which hit me very strongly was the way people were grieving for him. So many people had a very different and very personal grief because of my father's death. However, none of them were grieving because he was a rich man, neither were they grieving because he was a very resourceful man or because he was a very influential man. What struck me the most was that each one of them was grieving my father because my father made them happy! My father made each of them believe that they were very special every time he was with each of them.

Over the last three years, this has been my biggest struggle, to be like my father! I don't want to be remembered as a rich person or an influential person or a resourceful person but I would rather be remembered as a happy person, a person who spreads happiness, shares happiness!

However, I must acknowledge that this has been the toughest target I have set for myself so far. I had to do quite a lot of work and I'm still doing a lot of work to reach a stage where I can be happy, and share happiness with everybody who is with me. As a part of the last three years, I have had enormous amounts of dialogues with myself which you can call monologues! These dialogues have helped me realise what I really care for and what is important for me. I had to ask so many questions to reach this state of understanding. This book is to share my journey so far!

As a part of a career in HR, one is exposed to many ways of human development. I have spent hours with people figuring out how they look at their lives, what do they, why do they want it, and the like. I have done or witnessed many efforts to teach people how to talk, communicate, how to trust. But the basic fact is our biggest struggle is accepting ourselves! Understand ourselves! Most of the struggles I have witnessed are a result of this.

If I have to look my best, appear my best, I take help of a mirror. I stand in front of it and ensure that my hair are right, my dress looks good, my appearance is proper! On the other hand if my hand is paining or say, I have a serious headache what do I do? At some point I'll go to the doctor. The doctor would advise me on taking necessary tests may be an x-ray or scans etc, or may be any other kind of tests which may be relevant.

So, a mirror takes care of ensuring that my appearance is good and pathological tests ensure that my health is right.

But what will normally help me to ensure that my mind and my soul are in a good condition?

Then there are those who explore in knowing themselves. Spend time spiritually and get aware. If most of us are struggling to buy our happiness thru different "materials" some spirituals are trying to explore it within! However, for a very long time, I have struggled to understand what all these spiritual ways are and what do they mean to each one of us. I have been blessed with many seniors in the field as colleagues or as my superiors, as my bosses but I have to accept that I have given them a tough time when they tried to make me see beyond the obvious of my day-to-day life.

When I used to be with all these experts of spiritual development I used to, most times find myself lost for some reasons. I always used to have an impression that all these things were going away from one's "Active" life. Being spiritual is like the next stage of your development. When you are in an ongoing pursuit of life, these things actually do not make a lot of sense.

Many of my colleagues, bosses and friends have tried to have these conversations with me to make me realise that being spiritual is as a part of life as may be being a movie buff or may be of being a music lover. In the last three years, some of these conversations have helped me in the toughest times of my life. However, I used to actually push them away with a lot of reluctance. The interesting part is that I see many others doing the same. Not that each of us is so aware of these tools, techniques of processes, as they call them, to get closer to yourself and to understand yourself better and so make decisions for life in a more informed and better way.

My first effort was to find this peace for myself while continuing with my normal life. So I have been trying to think about a simple way to get closer to myself and to understand myself. I wanted a way which is more relevant to my personal struggles, my opinions and decisions. As a part of these explorations I stumbled upon few very basic realities and those helped me hugely. When I was trying to figure out why and how, then some time back I actually came down to writing down some questions which helped me understand myself better. These questions were a start for a few interesting conversations I has with myself. They brought me so much clarity and peace. They started with acceptance of my own self and moved ahead with creating space for some changes.

As they helped me, I was looking at a way to share it with all those who go through a similar struggle. Initially, I thought it could be a diary where every morning you address one of the questions and then think about it. Then you actually try and write down the answer. However, the more I thought of it, I realised that it was far more than just a diary or just a set of questions. I genuinely wanted the reader to think about these questions and ponder over them, analyse them and be with these questions and then actually answer them truthfully. That was how this idea for this book emerged.

Right from the beginning, I was clear that it had to be a simple book. A book about the pursuit of happiness in a normal life! It would be useful to those who do not have an opportunity or maybe do not feel the necessity, or maybe are not exposed to any of the spiritual awakening-simple people who live a normal life and deal with basic issues. Each of us has to face some situations in our lives commonly. There are ups and the downs and some highs and lows. We all need some sort of strength boosters. Many a time, we need help in just assuring that what we are doing is right!

The whole idea of this book is for those who probably are not very comfortable having these kinds of conversations with somebody else. The book is designed in such way that you will feel very comfortable about the journey you take here. So there is a discussion followed by a simple question. You are expected to answer these questions for yourself. The advantage it has is that you don't have to share these questions with any third person. Rather you have to answer it for yourself! It may not be done in partnership with someone. These are intended dialogues you have with your own self. That's why they are not just monologues but they are Mirrored Monologues! They will bring you immense power!

PURPOSE AND FORMAT OF THE BOOK

This book is written so you ask a few questions to yourself and really make an effort to find answers for them. It is an effort that each reader will make to get closer to own self and find a sense of acceptance! I guarantee that if you accept yourself for what you truly are, it would make you really happy and be at peace!

As I mentioned, this book is your own dialogue with your own self. Created as if you are asking a question to yourself and you are answering it for yourself. As it is a dialogue with the self there need not be any inhibitions or any kind of defensiveness or any kind of boundaries there. It is written in very simple language so that the vocabulary is not an impediment but rather it works as something which will catch your interest and make this entire journey easy on you.

More than a book, I would like to call this a journey, a journey of maybe of some 15 odd questions. I would strongly request each of my readers to treat it as a journey and not read it like a book in one sitting. The way this journey is designed has a certain format and I very sincerely request each of you to please allow that format to work for you. The temptation to read it in one go would be very high but again and again I will really request you to please let this journey happen to you rather than you make it happen by reading it in just one go.

It is also very easy to read this book and let it stay on your mind and just get on with your life as it is. But that would be just one part of this journey. You need to create space for your own self to actually take this journey ahead which means allow yourself an opportunity to really detach from your day-to-day chores and routine and really be with the question or be with the process or be with the content of this journey for some time at least. I do not want to make it sound very difficult or complex for you by saying that every day you have to do this and every day you need to do this. It's not that. But if your own self is telling you that you need to be alone and actually process whatever you are reading in this book please allow that space to yourself.

This journey would require two things from you. Flow and Format! Flow as in the readiness to start this journey and keep going on till you reach the final stage! Also trust the format to conclude the entire journey for you!

For anything which is about ourselves be it health or be it any kind of interest we want to pursue, the way our mind processes is, why do you want to do it or why do you want to do it now? A similar thing will happen when you take this journey or start on it. It is good to say that this is all nonsense and this is not of any use. Very commonly you may have 20 things going on in your life. You have your family to take care of, maybe some relationship, there is a job which is extremely high pressured and there are some deadlines in the project, and what not. I would suggest that any such point comes in this journey please don't think of entire 15 questions, just look beyond that one particular day. The important thing is to start. Finally, it is about knowing yourself. It is about exploring what your life is all about.

What it means is that it is your journey, so if you could not complete something today don't build a lot of guilt around it. Just promise yourself that I'll do it on the next possible moment and then do it! It is not a course at the end of it which you have to write any exam. By completing this you are not going to get any certificate from any third person.

The second thing is to trust the format and do not give up. There are very short chapters or sections of this journey. It is quite possible that you may not be convinced with some of them right away. However our request would be please allow the whole thing to happen. Don't give up in the middle just because it looks too simple.

At the end of each chapter a space is given. You may write your answers there. Please record your feelings, emotions, choices there freely. If that space is running short please use another notebook. You need not show what you write to anyone. But please ensure that you actually write down your answers.

If at any place the book is saying that you need spend some time with a particular question for couple of days, please do so. Please don't rush into solving it as any examination paper. Rather treat it like a nice journey of exploration.

In the end all what you're going to do is going to be forming a kind of a collage and creating a picture for your own self. The collage of your future life filled with things which make you happy along with people who bring your happiness, doing stuff which you like! Is this a good enough reason?

Now while doing all of these things they are certain tools which I have to suggest to each of you and I very sincerely request you to use these tools as a part of this journey.

TOOLS

SELF TALK: THE MIRRORED MONOLOGUES

It may sound very crazy. It may look very crazy. But this is one of the most effective tools of addressing your feelings and your emotions. When there is a question or when you're thinking about something, I request you to sit alone at any place which makes you comfortable and have a dialogue with yourself. Pretend that you are asking this question to yourself and pretend that there are two of "you"-one who is asking a question and one who is answering it.

Please understand that these self talks have to be like a conversation happening out loud. It may not be a very comfortable thought, so you need to have very comfortable surroundings to do this. If you need to be alone in the house, make it happen. If you need to go somewhere and sit with nature or in the garden, do that. Figure out what your requirement is and go with that. However, when you do these self talks, do it as a conversation and not as what is going on in your mind. These have to be loud conversations. Do not get confused with your own mind talking to you or the thought process which is going on in your head with the self talks. Self talks are conversations and dialogues and talks which you have with your own self. They need to be loud, they need to be private, and they need to be comfortable.

WRITING

Writing is another extremely powerful tool. I genuinely request you that whenever you've been told to write an answer for a certain question as a part of this journey, please follow it and write it down. Write it down in this book itself. There are spaces to write, but if you have something that needs to be written and is not fitting into the given space below, please use extra sheets or extra papers. Do not use computers, mobile phones and tabs. Try writing with a pen on paper! Even though, it looks like an ancient skill, it has great power to make you at peace.

As a part of this journey, you would have two types of thought processes. First would be about the questions that this journey is asking you. The second would be the emotions and feelings that the answers would create. Our suggestions to you would be that the first part would anyway get covered. As a part of this book, it would tell you where to write answers to the questions asked. However, for the second part which is about your emotions and feelings related to these questions, if you're not able to find space, use a different notebook to record them. Sometimes, writing down your emotions and feelings release a lot of negativity and sadness. At the end of writing it, you would feel so much at peace.

SELF-WALK

Another important tool through this journey is taking long walks with yourself, while thinking about questions asked in this journey. Just be with yourself and allow the contradicting thought processes too flow. These walks will help you get past them, rather than analysing or judging any of them.

Please ensure that you are alone on these walks. Let the main companion be your thoughts. You will be surprised to see how brilliantly your mind speaks if you choose to listen to it. So, if possible, avoid music or other noise. Let these be walks with your thoughts!

HOW COMMITTED ARE YOU TO TAKING THIS JOURNEY?

Let me start by telling you the story of a small boy.

There was a small village which was suffering from a drought for a few years at a stretch. The villagers decided to come together and offer prayers to the deity of the village. A day was fixed and the time was fixed at 5 o'clock, early in the morning. It was decided that all the villagers would gather in the temple on top of the village hill.

As agreed, everybody gathered there at 5 o'clock in the morning. Just when they were getting ready to start the prayers, a small boy joined them. He had an umbrella in hand. Everybody looked at him. Some started laughing at his stupidity as the village had not seen any rain in the last few years. Then, somebody asked the boy why he had brought the umbrella along. The boy looked puzzled and asked, "Are we not offering prayers to the deity so that it rains?"

So, do you have your umbrella?

How committed are you to take this journey? Please feel free to write down your responses. Please note your feelings and emotions. Make sure to look for any resistance that you may have towards this journey. Note any doubts, questions or reservations that you may have.

After writing it all down, go through your answers and please acknowledge your emotions.

PART 1

Acknowledge and Accept

DO YOU LIKE YOURSELF?

I had an interesting conversation with one of the young employees working in one of my previous places of employment. The conversation was about his performance improvement plan. As the HR Head of the organisation, I was supposed to talk to this employee and find out why his performance had slipped suddenly. This person had graduated from a rather prominent engineering college and had been working with our organisation for a couple of years. He was a consistent good performer. However, for six months, his performance was not up to the expected level and it had become a problem. I had to have a conversation with him.

The first thing which struck me while talking to him was the sadness I saw in his eyes. I did not want to make him uncomfortable so I started by generally asking about his life and what he is doing. It was evident that there was something bothering him in his life. Maybe it had an impact on his work. At one point, he broke down and said, "I'm so fed up of living up to the expectations of everyone around me. I actually don't want to do it anymore!" When he started talking, he started as a sad person but eventually when he talked a little more, there was a lot of anger in him. To cut a long story short, he was the perfect representative of the middle-class that wants their children to do well. A lot of emphasis is made on education, scoring good grades and finally actually getting a good job. Once the job starts, the struggle is about consistently being good at it and then getting a promotion and then growing further and getting a higher salary, being at par in the market and so on and so forth. We all know this.

So I asked him, "Are you telling me that you don't want to do well? What is it?" His answer was, "Of course, I want all of these things! I want a good life for myself, but at the same time I'm not sure if anyone cares about what I want. Everybody is so focused on results and outcomes and performance and achievements that my efforts are not seen by anyone. Not in the office, not at home-is anyone bothered about what my day is actually like?" He shared that he was an average student and did well by studying hard but he was never extraordinarily intelligent. He was not very good at art or any extracurricular activity. He was a normal guy living a normal, average life. But his life was not working for him. It was not making any sense.

I asked him, "Do you like yourself?" He was taken aback for a minute and then emphatically said, "Yes. But what do you mean by that? Of course I like myself..." I said, "I mean, do you like yourself? Do you like yourself physically and emotionally? Do you like the kind of intelligent person that you are, the value system you have, your thinking process, how you react to things, and your opinions about your social circle, your communication style...?" He was suddenly silent and after maybe a couple of minutes, he answered, "I am not too sure..."

Does it not sound like a very common story? I am not sure what I like about myself. I don't know why I like it. If I am asked about three blunders of my life, I can count five! But if I am asked about three achievements of my life... then? Can I call my 10th Standard Exam result my achievement? Or can I say tha getting a job with a good MNC is my achievement? What is my achievement? It makes me so uncomfortable. Why?

Sometimes the irony is that somebody else has to show you what is good in you. Personally you never spend any time in exploring what you like about being yourself. If you are not even spending time to acknowledge it, how can you nurture it? How can you protect it? If you do not compliment yourself, how can you compliment others? And more so, why would others compliment you?

Please write your thoughts here.

What do you like about your appearance? What do you dislike about it?

What do you like about yourself beyond your appearance? What do you dislike?

Why do you like or dislike a particular thing?

DO YOU LIKE YOUR LIFE?

Very recently, I conducted an online survey on one a social networking site. The survey had very limited questions. One of the questions was, "Are you happy with your life?" It was an objective question and there were three options given as answers-yes, no or can't say. Over 200 people answered this survey for me.

It was amazing to see that approximately 30% of my respondents replied saying that they were happy with their lives. Another 40% clearly replied saying that they were not happy with their lives. Another 30% respondents were in the last category. They replied saying that they couldn't say whether they were happy or unhappy about their lives.

What makes us happy in life? Is it the car we drive or the house we live in, the organisation we work for, the clothes we wear, the brands we accessorise? What is it? If we look deep within ourselves, the answer is very simple. The only time we feel happy is when we are at peace within. Peace within our heart is a tricky thing, isn't it? Because, what makes me peaceful could be different from what makes someone else peaceful.

One very common discussion is about materialistic things and non-materialistic things and their places in our happiness. I would want to put this debate at rest for this journey. Each of us has complete freedom to decide what makes us peaceful and happy! What brings smile to my face could be varied-from a BMW car to 30-minutes playtime with my child. In some cases it could be both!

But then, that's the fun! We all get to choose what we want to say! And guess what? These are your Mirrored Monologues. There is no judgement, no raised eyebrow, and no arguments.

This means that you don't have to compromise on acknowledging your dreams, aspirations, values, beliefs, emotions and feelings. Surprisingly, it is never only about emotions and feelings or about dreams and aspirations. It's a combination of all of it!

Normally, the dreams and aspirations are addressed because one has to make decisions about which job to take, what salary to accept, what project to work on, and so on and so forth. But when it comes to emotions and feelings or values and beliefs, we don't acknowledge them and do not make any efforts to do things which will makes this part of us happy!

It is so amusing that even though you may be having your dream job earning the best on the market while working for one of the best teams, if you are not respected as a human being or if your organisation does not have the kind of value system that you have or if your emotions and feelings are not finding a way out, you are unhappy about your life. It is important to note that the car you drive to office, the office you go to, the phone you use-all these things just add to a certain part of your happiness. But if you do not find time to express your love for your family or to do fun things with your children or maybe have a nice cup of coffee over some light-hearted chit chat with your friends, all these things mentioned above will not be sufficient.

It is the freedom to choose the life that you want, which makes you happy. However, how many times have you asked yourself what kind of life you want to live? Does it have to be so hectic? Does it have to be so stressful? Does it have to be so away from your family? Does it have to be so dry and ruthless? What kind of life do you want?

The most powerful part about all these self dialogues is that it actually wants you to believe that you do have a choice and you can change your life!

But before you get up and start changing things in your life, you actually need to know what it is that you want to change. Personally, I'm uncomfortable about any kind of change just for the sake of change. I feel one of the major reasons why there is resistance to change is that most times, some part of the change is not required by those who are putting up a fight. Even though I support change in life, at the same time, I have come to realise that there are things which should not change in my life. At the same time, if something has to change, it should have a proper reason behind it.

My request at this stage to you would be not to bother about changing things but rather focus on why and what needs to be changed. The thought process at this point should be focused on what is making me happy and what is making me unhappy. The self dialogues at this stage need to ask yourself the likes and dislikes and elaborate the reasons behind them. Please respect the need for privacy at this stage, because only then, you will be able to answer truthfully.

Please answer here. Do you like your life? What do you like? What do you dislike in your life? If you are given a choice, what would you want to change?

DO YOU LIKE PEOPLE AROUND YOU?

I've always lived with the habit of accommodating a lot of people in my life. Sometimes, many of these people have taken advantage of this. I had formed the habit of accommodating people's expectations in my life, over the years. This habit grew into a stage where my life was filled with things that I had to do for many people around me. These people are my own people-they were my family, my friends, my colleagues and bosses. I'm very good at planning and organising things in my life, so I always have extra time. I'm never pressed for targets and deadlines, and it's very rare that I don't have time. Unfortunately, people around me started believing that I had too much free time. I'm talking about a time when I had a very hard-pressing job as the HR Head of an organisation and I had a four-year-old daughter, and a household to take care of. I love to cook, I love to help people-and so, I ended up getting up at 4:00 AM and staying up late, after 11:00 PM just to ensure that everyone around me was happy.

It was surprising that in this entire period, no one was happy and the biggest loser was me! Over the years, many people around me got into the habit of using me. They would call at any odd hour to discuss their problems with me or would ask me to accompany them to do things I didn't want to do. But when I turned around to ask for help for my problems, most of them were too busy or had something of their own to deal with. I could never understand why this was happening to me.

On the professional front, a similar pattern was seen. On the one hand, I was praised for my performance. On the other hand, I was continuously taken for granted. My sense of fairness was so evident that no one around me was afraid of me being stupid or irrational at any given point. The result? No one felt the need to take care of me. Everyone around me felt that I could help them.

It was making me so miserable inside, but I didn't realise it. When I planned a dinner at my place, my so-called close friends used to turn up late. My boss could just forget to mention my contribution in a very important meeting. Though my image was that of an aggressive and dominating person, in my heart I was killing myself for not being able to say no, for letting people take me for granted, and for allowing my so-called good friends mistreat me.

When I look around, I see so many people going through a similar problem. Remember, during our school days, we wanted to be a part of a particular group that we actually took so much nonsense from them just to be able to hang out with them? We ignored a person who admired us for what we were and chose to be with someone who had an opinion about what we should be. When we were growing up, just to be a part of the happening crowd, we accepted a boyfriend or a girlfriend who never valued us. Once we grew up and started working, we allowed our bosses to make fun of us in public places. We allowed our colleagues to take credit for the work we put in.

The worst part of all this is that it is my energy which gets killed every time I make one of these mistakes. There are so many people around me who want me to believe that the only way to glory in my life is by satisfying them. These people are the source of most of my unhappiness!

I remember talking to a technocrat who was known for his brilliant mind and sincerity, when he was going through a bad phase of his life. His girlfriend for four years had dumped him. This 5'6" tall guy with a very ordinary appearance and an extraordinary brain was a gold medallist from one of the top technical institutes of India was cursing himself because so-called love of his life chose a taller and better looking guy over him. It took me almost two hours to make this amazing guy realise that no one in this world has a right to make him feel so miserable and that probably he needs to look for someone who values him for what he is.

It's just not my or this guy's example. Every time I have tried to help someone to find reasons behind their unhappiness, their problems or sorrows, most often, the reasons have been centred on a person or a few people in their lives. It is high time that we look around and identify people around us. Who around me makes me happy and why? Who around me makes me unhappy and why?

There is a beautiful Zen story. Once, in a room full of people, there was a huge elephant standing. Everyone was uncomfortable because of the lack of space. Everybody could see the elephant and realise that the lack of space was because of the elephant in the room. But no one chose to say anything. If I treat my mind like a room and all the negativity or unhappiness as the elephant, I need to acknowledge the space it is taking up. I need to push it out of the room, which means that I need to push all this negativity out of my mind to create space for things and people that make me happy.

Let us not treat this as a movie script to identify the good and the bad guy or girl for that matter. This is your life and so you need to differentiate people you don't like and things you don't like.

Let me give you an example. I hate being late, I hate those who are late for anything. Imagine coming from a country where there is the concept of Indian Standard Time, I cannot stand a delay of even five minutes! I can't understand how someone can be late-if you have given your time to someone, you better adhere to it. If you're getting late, inform them in advance. One of my very close friends is always late. Not only that, she does not feel bad about it. I hate this habit of hers but I love her. Every time I talk to her, she helps me to see a point, she listens to me every time I need to talk, she's always there, she creates space for me to do things which she does not like, and she does not judge me for those things. I can accommodate her coming late. But somebody else who does not give me similar comfort cannot demand that I tolerate their being late.

It is a belief that, as you cannot see yourself, you see yourself only through others. But the way a mirror reflects opposites, what you see in others the most is what you do not like about yourself. Is that too heavy? Let's make it simpler. What it means is, what you do not like about someone is actually inside you and it comes back to you through someone else. For the time being, the easiest way to deal with it is to acknowledge it. Whether it is with someone else or whether it is inside you. Let's not spend too much time in locating it right now. Let's take a moment to acknowledge things you like and do not like.

Please think about it. Think about who around you adds to your happiness and how they do that. What are the things that the people around you do to add to your happiness?

Think about who makes you unhappy and how they make you unhappy.

Please write down your answers.

DO YOU TRUST OTHERS? DO OTHERS TRUST YOU?

I once conducted a training program for some middle-level managers of a manufacturing company, which means that their age group was somewhere around mid to late 30s. The discussion was about how to assert oneself and how to say no. There was an intense discussion about why we are worried about saying no. Suddenly, we stumbled upon something very beautiful called "TRUST."

I asked a question to all my participants. How many people in their lives do they trust completely? This had to be complete trust, about every aspect of their life. How many people did they trust? The answer on an average was two or three people around them.

My next question was how many people around them trust them in a similar way? The average answer was that the same people they trust, trusted them back.

Now the group had this huge reality in front of them that in the average 37 years of their lives they had only two or three people around them who they trusted and who trusted them. Is it not a scary thought that you don't have enough people around you to trust?

Due to the lack of trust, apart from those few people around you, the rest of them are looked at with some doubt. Your energy is going into hiding some aspect of your life from many people around you. If you are in a bad mood and need to talk, you need to wait to be with one of these few people to lay your guard down. If you are going through problems at work, you need to invest so much of your energy in hiding it from so many other people.

Let me tell you a story. Once a father and son were playing and the son wanted to jump from a higher place, but was scared. The father kept encouraging him to jump but he was obviously very scared. So the father said, "Don't worry son! I'll hold you!" The son said, "No, what happens if you don't catch me?" The father said, "Don't worry, I will catch you!" The son said, "Are you sure?" The father answered, "Yes, I am sure I will catch you!" The son jumps and the father does not catch him. The son falls and hurts himself. Crying, and angry, the son looks at his father and says, "You said you will catch me!" The father looks at him and says, "This will teach you never to trust anyone. You should always look out for yourself!"

We are trained to not to trust. The lack of trust actually puts pressure on each of us. We are so sure that most people around us either wish us bad or are jealous of us or do not care. Just because we have a few bad experiences, we let it affect our judgement so much that we are scared of trusting! So much of our energy goes in searching for proof of why we should not trust anyone. We don't trust, we teach our children not to trust and the cycle goes on.

How do we decide if someone is worthy of our trust or not? Are there any set patterns? To trust that someone understands me, do I look for someone who is a good listener or someone who has a similar story like mine? But what happens if both these traits are not present in someone, do I assume that he or she won't be trustworthy?

To an extent, I can understand that to trust completely with all aspects of all our lives we need people who we know for a long time and maybe who have proved in the past that they are on our side. But what about simple things like being myself? Can I have more people around me with whom I can think of being myself, where I don't have to pretend?

The most important fact to understand here is that trusting others relieves us of pressure. It allows us to believe that others are not here to harm us all the time and so we don't need to look out for ourselves all the time. I can spend time on other things in life. I can be fun, as not everyone is here to make fun of me. I can be relaxed as not everyone here is to make my life complicated.

One more extension of this discussion would be that even if you are accepting that there are a few people you trust or who trust you, how much time are you spending with them? For how much time can you afford to be yourself and not waste energy in projecting yourself as somebody else? How much of your stress is coming out of the fact that there are such few people around you who you trust? Can you feel that tension right now? Can you see the time you spend in this stress and how it has become part of your life? It has become a habit.

Please write here: How many people in your life do you trust completely? How many people trust you completely? How frequently do you spend time with each of these people? If possible, write down examples of why you would not trust someone easily. What stops you from trusting? What makes you trust? What are the signals you look for?

____

____

____

____

WHAT IS YOUR ENERGY PATTERN?

During my hostel days, when it was time for the examinations, you could see two main patterns. Some of us would stay up until late at night to study, perhaps until 2:00 or 2:30 AM. Some of us would get up at 2:30 or 3:00 AM and then study all morning. It was funny that both groups used to find it difficult to understand how the other did it. Those who stayed late could never understand how one could wake up so early and those who woke up early could never understand how one could stay up late.

All through our life, we have such patterns about our energy levels and our preferences. Even when we start work, we have a favourite time of the day when most of our work gets done. However, over the years, we lose track of our energy pattern and just try and accommodate whatever is convenient. Let's see, if you can log your energy and its patterns for the next four-five days. Let us look at the following format and see if you can log in your energy patterns, record them and then let's see what they each tell you.

ENERGY LOG

	Day 1	Day 2	Day 3	Day 4	Day 5	Example
7:00 AM						8
9:00 AM						7
11:00 AM						7
2:00 PM						4 (had a heavy lunch)
4:00 PM						5
6:00 PM						7
8:00 PM						7

Scale to refer–0–10

0 implies very Low energy, feeling sleepy, tired and being unable to do anything 10 implies very high energy, feeling happy and fit to do any good work.

** Please note the times when your energy is below 5 or above 7. Please note down the reason behind this sudden rise or dip in the energy. Did you meet anyone? Did you talk to somebody? Did you do something specific?

It is interesting to see the pattern in your energy fluctuations. Some may find mornings to be the time when the energy is at its highest. Some may find it to be the afternoons or evenings. Let us note your own understanding and assessment of your energy log to conclude it and derive the patterns.

MY ENERGY REFLECTOR

Please put a dot for the respective score under the related columns. Join the dots for a particular day to get a graphical pattern of your energy

	Mornings (7:00 AM to 11:00 AM)	**Afternoons (2:00 PM to 4:00 PM)**	**Evenings (6:00 PM to 8:00 PM)**	**Scale**
Example			7	9
				6
				3
				0
Day 1				9
				6
				3
				0
Day 2				9
				6
				3
				0
Day 3				9
				6
				3
				0
Day 4				9
				6
				3
				0
Day 5				9
				6
				3
				0

Our inner energy defines our state of mind or in simpler words, our mood. How many times have you really sat down to understand what things kill your energy or things that actually suck out your energy. It is so interesting that there are certain things or people who actually suck out our energy every time we talk to them or meet them. Let's call these things and people "Energy Vampires."

These things or people actually suck out our energy. It is such a silent killer that we don't even realise that we're getting killed or our energy is getting killed. Every time we do a particular thing, our energy is killed. For example, every time I watch a horror movie, I get depressed, scared and traumatised for days. I can't think rationally and get scared. I can't sleep well. Horror movies are my energy vampires. The next logical step would be that I stop watching horror movies.

But the interesting part is that it is not always as simple as just watching horror movies. The energy vampires are not such simple things. It could be something like spending time with a particular relative or maybe talking on the phone with a certain close friend or it could be about spending half-an-hour listening to your boss or it could be something like sitting and watching television for hours, or it could be just an obsessive thought. The energy vampire could be anybody or could be anything.

You need to identify your energy vampires for yourself to actually stop being with that vampire. Let's take a moment and list down your observations about it. Please look at your energy log and reflector to note when your energy was very low and what caused that particular low energy. Was it a phone call? Was it a conversation? Was it an action? What actually caused the low energy? Let us look for some patterns. Can you identify any of your "Energy Vampires?"

Now let's come to the other part. What gets you high? Let's call them your "Energy Boosters!"

I love to cook. If I spend 30 minutes in the kitchen cooking something for my family, it lifts my mood and my energy immediately. For me, early mornings and fresh air are also amazing energy boosters.

Let's look at the log again and understand when your energy was very high. What were you doing then? Who were you with? Was a particular kind of music playing? Were you exercising? Were you eating a particular kind of food? What is boosting your energy? Let's take a moment to identify your "Energy Boosters!"

Do you see a pattern of the part of the day in which your energy is very high? Is there any relation to what you are choosing to do, with a particular part of the day? Please take a moment to register your observations.

Think about your energy vampires and energy boosters and the amount of time you spend on each. Where is your maximum time going? Does it go in doing things which make you energetic or which make you dull? What can you do about it?

DO YOU FEEL HEALTHY?

For the last five years I've had a weight problem. My clothes size went from medium to large to extra large and now, to extra extra large. Do I know I have a weight problem? Of course I know I have a weight problem. Don't I understand that what the extra weight would do to my health? Of course I understand! Why am I not choosing to do anything about it?

For the last couple of years, my priorities were very different. I used to work early in mornings and then finish my day early to spend evenings with daughter. My husband would start late and take care of our daughter's morning schedule and then work till late at night. I am sure many of you would have a similar story. The result was the only time we got together as a family would go into doing family things. We spent all our free time with each other. So in a way I made a choice that the focus would be my family time!

At least that is what I was telling myself! However the reality is that I do not like exercising! I understand that it is a necessity of life and to live a healthy and active life, you need to be in proper shape and you need to exercise. I am a fat person. I am a person who loves food of all kinds. I do not want to bother about what is healthy and what is not so healthy. I love tasty food how unhealthy it is. I cannot eat food which does not have taste or flavour just because it is healthy. But that's who I am. Now what does that mean? It means my health cannot be dependent on the food I eat, or, I need to figure out a way to maintain proper metabolism! Period!

I'm sure that each of you would have your own perception of health, weight, your appearance, and what you want to do about it. I want you to take a minute to just give yourself a space and accept that it is your choice. Say it aloud, "My health is my choice!" You are not bound by any so-called social fads of how you should look, what size you should be or what your height to weight ratio should be. Your health is not governed by any of these things. Remember? "My health is my choice!" Please take a moment to allow yourself the space where there is no judgement about any of these things. None of these things define you or the kind of a person that you are.

My health has to be something beyond the superficial. You cannot starve yourself and be happy. You cannot overeat and be happy. You cannot be hungry physically and be content mentally. At the same time, you cannot be overstuffed and feel energetic. Even if you eat less or eat more, in both cases you get acidity. What does that mean? My body needs balance! A balance between how much to eat and how to digest it. You need to differentiate what food would make you happy emotionally and what food will make your body happy physically.

How much ever you go to the gym and exercise or bicycle, it will just take care of a certain part of your health. If by staying at size zero will make me constantly irritated or irritable or shout at people around me or, have less gratitude towards life or everyone around me, that figure is as unhealthy as being overweight.

Our body has immense intelligence. We should learn to listen to our body. It will tell you when to eat and when to stop eating. It will tell you what it likes and what it does not like. We should just choose to listen to that wisdom! So many studies say that your emotional health and your physical health are connected with each other.

The first secret is that health is my choice! The second secret is my health is about my emotional and my physical well-being combined together!

Now let's listen to our body's wisdom and first understand what is working and what is not working.

Please ask yourself what you like about your physical health and why you like it. What is it that about your physical health that you dislike? Why do you dislike it? What is it that about your emotional health that you like and why do you like it? What is it that about your emotional health that you dislike and why do you dislike it?

Please take a moment to process these answers. Please remember once again that it is your choice. Allow yourself the freedom and then choose to answer these questions.

HOW DO YOU RELATE TO OUR SOCIETY?

In my residential complex, every evening, some of us bring our children down to the play area, to play. Unfortunately in our complex, the driveway and the play area are not separate. So many times, there is an incident of somebody driving very fast and all the children getting scared or mothers getting scared for the safety of their children. Every time a car is seen entering fast in society, mothers and kids start shouting and mothers start gossiping amongst each other about how so-and-so is driving so fast and how so-and-so is not bothered about children playing downstairs. Very few of us actually go to the driver and explain it to him, and tell him why is it important that he drives slowly once he enters the society.

A friend of mine has this habit of going to the driver and telling him or her in detail about how there are children riding bicycles, that toddlers are in their toddler cars, there are children who run around and are all in their own world. They are not bothered about whether there is a car coming or whether there is a bike coming, or if somebody's driving fast. She tells him that they are not the driver's children but as a mother, she requests him to be more careful and allow her child and the other children to play. Then she asks if they can please do that. The moment this is explained to the person who is driving fast, in a majority of the cases, people understand and the next time, they are careful.

However, if we just choose to talk amongst each other and not bother to explain it to the driver, things will not change. This may look like a silly example of a silly problem. But it is an example of situations we are in and how we choose to react to these situations. As this problem is related to my fear of the safety of my child, I am affected by it.

In a similar way, there are many things around us which keep affecting us. Consciously or subconsciously, all these matters which happen in our office or in society or in our community or politically in our nation or world over, is affecting us. It is affecting our opinions and choices in life. Very rarely do we sit down and acknowledge this impact which these things have on our lives.

Every time around the elections, all social networking sites will be full of political opinions. I am sure even you have one. That is not what we are talking about. We are talking about issues like increasing crime around us, decreasing a sense of safety for girls or kids, traffic situations, mistreatment to elders, corruption, lack of any value system and the like. I agree with the theory of the circle of concern and the circle of control. I'm not asking you to mix these two. This is not about trying to resolve a social issue or trying to resolve a situation in the office or trying to resolve the traffic problems of my country. No it's not about that! At least not at this stage.

At this stage, this is only about acknowledging the impact of all these things on my life. What irritates me the most? What causes me worry? It is about accepting how these situations around us impact us and how our decisions are sometimes a result of that impact.

Please look around and ask yourself how do you feel about your surrounding? How do you feel about the value system of the place where you work? How do you feel about the way your community is? How do you feel about the political situation in your country? How do you feel about the job market in the world? How do you feel about the overall way of life that the world is following?

What are your opinions about all of these worldwide issues? Just take a moment to acknowledge things which you are consciously or subconsciously noticing and letting them impact your choices.

WHO DRIVES YOUR LIFE?

Now we enter one of the scariest zones of our mind. The fears! What are my fears?

Have you heard the story of the rabbit?

There was a rabbit who was scared that the sky would fall on his head. I know that those who read ASTERIX comics are familiar with this phenomenon.

Let's come back to this rabbit. So this rabbit is scared that the sky is going to fall on his head. He runs and runs and runs. Then, he finds a place under a huge tree and thinks that if the sky falls, it will fall on the tree and that he will be safe. Then suddenly, a leaf falls on his head and guess what happens? The rabbit thinks that the sky has started falling. He starts shouting and running everywhere. He starts telling everyone to run as the sky is falling. He scares everybody around him. All the animals in the jungle who hear him are scared to death as the sky is falling. The king of the jungle, the big lion comes and asks what is wrong. "Why is everyone panicking? What happened?" Everybody says that the sky is falling! The King asks, "Who told you?" Everyone said, "The rabbit!" The King asked the rabbit, "Who told you that the sky is falling?" The rabbit says, "A piece of sky fell on my head!" The King asks, "What piece?" The rabbit says, "It's on my head!" The king looks at him and everybody looks at him. They see what's on his head. They see the leaf and start laughing!

Some of us live our lives like that rabbit. We are constantly worried that the sky is going to fall, that something bad is going to happen. We don't want to trust anyone. We don't want to ask anyone to check. We just are scared. So scared!

What are these fears? They are fears related to safety, maybe emotional, economical, and social. Fears can be related to death, diseases. Fears can be related to relationships, jobs, investments and the like. But how are these fears affecting us?

Let me tell you about a friend of mine who was going through a lot of marital problems. She was going through a miserable time and used to cry a lot and used to be very unhappy. Once when I was talking to her, I was trying to find out what was causing problems in their marriage? Theirs was a love marriage and even then, there was such a lack of communication, such a lack of companionship, such a lack of sharing and I was not able to see why that would happen. I asked a lot of questions about what she shared with her husband or what he shared with her. In that conversation, I was surprised at some of the answers she gave me.

She said she was sick and tired of taking care of herself and ensuring that she looked her best every day and every moment! I asked her why she was doing it and her answer was that otherwise, her husband would lose interest in her. "If I don't even look good why would he even look at me?" I asked her, "Is looking good so essential for your marriage?" She said, "Yes! Because that's the only way you can attract a man!" I said, "At what age?"

I want to believe that when you grow up past your 20s and your hormones are in a little more control, the physical beauty stops being THE attraction point. I mean, of course you want your spouse to look good and be healthy, and be well, but at the same time, marriage has to be beyond just that! That's my belief. Coming back to this friend of mine, she was saying that she spent too much of her energy on maintaining her looks because she believed that she had to look good to keep her marriage alive. Her "fear" was that if she stopped looking good, her husband would stop taking interest in her.

One more example comes to my mind. I used to have a colleague who was very shrewd. He would always know which side to butter up. He would go out of his way to compliment his boss. He would sometimes do some personal chores for the boss. Once, in a casual surrounding, someone teased him about it. His defence was that he did have the necessary educational background like all his colleagues. He climbed up the ladder only by hard work. He was not sure what would happen to him if his boss stopped favouring him. His "fear" was that he is not good enough compared to his colleagues so he would lose opportunities.

I want you to take a minute to read both these stories again and understand a pattern in it. There is a fear inside us which makes us believe a certain thing and then it actually results in a particular action. For example, my fear of losing a job will make me believe that I need to do anything to stay in the job. This means that I could be rude to people, start taking credit for another's work, start being mean to others. I could be so scared of my child's safety that I start fearing everything around me. I start believing that only I know what is best for my child and only I'm concerned about my child's well-being that I actually stop trusting everyone around me and start pushing everyone away. What does it mean? It means fears give birth to a belief and that results in action. Do you know what it means?

My fears are driving my life!

It is a scary thought. Allow yourself time to process this discussion. Please think about it in solitude and be truthful to yourself.

First of all, each of your fears is equally genuine and you have a right to feel them! You don't need to defend yourself for having these fears. They are your fears! First just acknowledge them.

What are your deepest fears? The fears which drive you crazy? What are the fears which make you stay awake at 3:00 AM? What fears define what you should or should not do in your life? Please make note of each of your fears.

ACKNOWLEDGE AND ACCEPT!

We have looked inside and we have asked ourselves so many questions. We have looked outside and done the same. Now what? If you've completed this journey so far, you will find yourself in a very restless place. Allow that restlessness to come up, because we're going to build on it!

I want you to go back to all your answers and read through them. I want you to see if there are any patterns in your answers. Do you see connections in who you like and who you dislike and what you like and what you dislike with what your energy vampires and what your energy boosters are?

Do you see a connection between your emotional health and things which you like and dislike? Do you see a connection between your fears and your thoughts about your social surroundings?

If your answers are truthful, and if you have had real self dialogues, at this point, you will find that each of these things is connected with the other. You will see a pattern in how your fears affect you and how they make you be with someone you don't like or they make you do a certain thing which makes you unhappy. You will see a pattern in how you like being with certain people and how it has a connection with one of your energy boosters.

Please see if there is any such pattern of these things and identify them. Make peace with them.

So far, this journey was about acknowledging and accepting what you are. Before we go further in this journey, you really need to make peace with all the choices you have made so far in life. You need to make peace with all your preferences about your life and how you have chosen to act or to how you chose to act away from your likes and your dislikes in your life.

Please spend at least a day or two in this restlessness of realisation of all these choices you've made in your life. Please spend time to have some self dialogues and accept whatever comes up. The choices you have made, the people you are with and how they impact you, the things which occupy your time and how you feel at the end of it-it all needs to be first acknowledged and accepted.

Before you take any further step in this journey, please ensure that you have had enough self dialogues to reach a state of acceptance or at least a beginning of that acceptance. Give yourself a right to feel restless, to feel agitated and to desire to start changing things in your life! Acknowledge the energy which is pushing you towards starting to change things around you. It will say, I know what I don't like, *so* let me stop it, I know what to do let me do it!

It is natural to feel that you know all the answers. But this journey was never about finding answers. It was actually about asking the right questions! The answers are there. But let's finish asking all the questions before we pick and choose the answers.

Right now, it is about just acknowledging and accepting!

HOW COMMITTED ARE YOU ON THIS JOURNEY?

You have completed the first section of this journey.

Let's take a moment and think about how this journey was so far. This would be the right opportunity to evaluate your commitment to this journey. How committed do you feel at this stage? Read your answer about commitment right in the beginning of the book. Have any of your feelings changed since then? Have you found any answers to the questions you raised then?

At this point, you will surely feel emotional about the answers you have given so far. This is the time to make a commitment to complete this journey, till the end, before you let your thoughts derail you. At this point, if you have any reservations or any questions, or any concerns for the journey ahead, please take a moment to think about it.

How committed are you feeling about the journey ahead? Are there still any questions or concerns in your mind?

PART 2

Choose to Nurture

WHAT IS YOUR LEGACY?

Let's start the second part of this journey in a slightly different way. Let us ask ourselves three questions before we say anything further. Please ensure that you spend enough mirrored monologues on these questions. It is time to take some time off with yourself and do some genuine thinking.

What is the legacy that you want to leave after you go? In simpler words, if you are told to pass on three of your personality traits to your children, what would you choose? What three characteristics of your personality are worth preserving and passing on to somebody else? Why would you choose these particular traits?

If your spouse or your partner is to choose three of his or her personality traits what should he or she pick? In other words, if your spouse or your partner has to pass on three of his or her personality traits to your children or to leave behind as the legacy what would you recommend he or she chooses? Why would you recommend those traits?

Whether you have it or not, in your opinion what are the general characteristics which future generations should have? What are the three traits that your children should have which neither you nor your spouse possess? Why do you think those are important?

What is a legacy? Legacy is something we are proud of leaving behind. Like education is the legacy left behind by the earlier generations. A classical Hindustani singer will leave his music as a legacy to the generations to come. All the scientific innovations are legacies of those innovators. What is our legacy?

Is our legacy limited only to the materialistic things we create? The assets we leave behind? The bank balance we have? Or can our legacy be beyond that?

We have complete freedom to decide what legacy we want to leave behind. Let it be more than just the assets and money. Can we leave our wisdom our knowledge and our character as a legacy? That's what my father did. He left behind his way of life as an example. I learned so much from it. I learned that I wanted to be a happy person, sharing happiness and this happiness would be my legacy.

We can leave only those things behind which we are proud of. That's what we leave behind for our children. We want them to have those things which we completely believe in.

It is a fact that based on our life experiences, and our stories, we paint a picture for our children. Whatever we think we couldn't do in our lives we want our children to do. We want our children to have all those qualities which we think we didn't have and if we would have had, our lives would have been better. It is so amazing to see that we want all these things for our children because we believe that we cannot have them. We are so sure that we cannot correct our lives now!

What if we change this belief? Let's decide that the correction can happen in my own life. The three things which you chose to be passed on to your children or to leave behind as the legacy are the three things which you surely want to nurture in your life. What if I tell you that the entire universe is conspiring for you to nurture those qualities? What if those are the things you need to focus on in your life ahead?

The legacy which you have chosen for your children is your incomplete quest in your life. Please spend some time on this thought. Go through your earlier answers and see how you need to fill your own life with those traits which you have mentioned as the desired traits for your children.

WHAT MAKES YOU LAUGH TILL YOU HAVE TEARS IN YOUR EYES?

I remember when I was a child, my sister and I used to laugh till we cried. We used to laugh for such silly things, things which actually have no meaning. But we could laugh our guts out at them. I remember getting scolded by my mother not for anything else but for my act of giggling for no reason. As a teenager, I remember sitting in a classroom, attending a boring class on physics or chemistry and trying to suppress the giggles just for a silly thing that the professor said, or something that my friend was trying to show me or some silly cartoons another friend would be drawing. Where has that laughter gone? When was the last time that I actually laughed till tears rolled down my cheeks?

Laughter is a sign of spontaneity. It is a sign of childlikeness, and a sign of light heart. Laughter is a sign of a positive state of mind. Where has that laughter gone? To see my young daughter having these giggles all the time, I find myself asking, *What* is so funny? She doesn't bother to answer because she knows I won't understand. Where are my giggles?

I kept thinking that why children can laugh so easily whereas most of the grown-ups cannot. If we accept that laughter is about spontaneity, why can't grown-ups be spontaneous? With every new role in our life we kind of put on a robe! A robe of intelligence, robe of grown-ups, robe of maturity, robe of being a software professional, robe of being a manager, robe of being a vice president, robe of being a mother, robe of being grandparent, and robe of being an adult, so many types of robes! Each of those robes takes away our spontaneity. Even if we want to laugh, that robe is a deterrent. It stops us from being spontaneous. "What is wrong with you? Have you lost your mind? Why are you laughing like this?" Do these things sound familiar? Do you have to laugh only when you lose your mind? "I'm so intelligent, I'm so rational! My reasoning is so strong. How can you laugh about something so illogical? I'm such a senior person I am superior to everybody else. They look up to me. How can I laugh at some stupid things?" Do these things sound familiar?

Each of the robes adds a deterrent in our spontaneity. We don't laugh. Then, this forms the habit of not laughing, but at the most, offering a smile or a smirk.

Just for once, let us get rid of some of these robes and try to be ourselves. Let us borrow some giggles from the younger ones around us. Let's try and be without any of these tags of being intelligent or matured or logical and find humour around us. Can you laugh now? Can you laugh your heart out–and have tears after the laughter? Can you break this habit of seriousness? Can you develop a habit of being playful, being childlike, being spontaneous, being yourself?

When was the last time that you laughed till you cry? What was it about? Which robes were absent at that moment?

WHO BRINGS A SMILE TO YOUR FACE EVERY TIME?

I remember going through a very bad phase in my career some time ago. I used to work for a company and my direct supervisor was a very insensitive man. He made it very difficult for me to work for him and I was finding it very difficult to go to office and bear the ignorance and the neglect he was showing me. He used to directly talk to my team and confuse them about my capabilities and my leadership. He took all the credit for all the work I did and while doing so, he actually portrayed me as an incompetent person. Half his achievements came through my hard work but not only that-he chose to ignore my hard work and also decided to sidetrack me for whatever reason.

For almost four-and-a-half months, I went through a miserable time and going to office was terrible. Every day, I would find that he had done something to put me in a difficult spot. Sometimes, it would be a direct conversation with him or something he said to my team members or sometimes it would be a one-line email which he had sent about a simple issue to be blown out of proportion, or he chose to disregard my emails where I had tried to share some of my work with him. I knew that this was not working and I had to take a decision, but somehow, I was not arriving at the decision. During this entire period, going to office was the most difficult thing to do in the whole world, for me.

It was very stressful! There were times when I'd just wanted to throw something on this guy's head or maybe slap him across the face or maybe go and ask the superior bosses how could you let this happen? I wanted to ask my CEO, "Are you blind?" But of course I could not do any of those things.

Surprisingly, despite all these tensions and the negativity and all this bitterness, I was actually not very sad! All this was a very superficial phenomenon for me. Nothing was at a deeper level!

How did I manage it? I used to do a simple thing every time I felt let down by my boss or feel miserable because of what he had said or done. Practically every time I was in a bad state, I just visualised my daughter's face in front of me: the picture of her doing something mischievous or maybe her smile or her eyes looking at me with all the drama in the world. It used to bring such a nice smile on my face! I used to think of her and forget the bad things around me. Her smile and all the bitterness would melt away.

I did not have a picture of her on my machine or desk. It was just a visualisation of her face. It would bring such a wonderful smile on my face. I was sure that each of us has somebody who brings a smile on our faces every time we think of them.

Who brings a smile to your face every time you think of them?

How often you think of this person? When you are gloomy, do you make an effort to remember this person? How much time you spend on this person?

WHAT MAKES YOU SICK IN YOUR GUT?

In one of the process labs I had attended, our group comprised eight of us, from very different backgrounds and age groups. Some of you would know the structure of process labs, where you put a group in a comfortable surrounding with a facilitator who will only facilitate conversations. There are no judgements, there are no skills sessions or any management games but just the discussions where the whole group is involved. From these discussions participants tend to find answers to some of their issues.

So, as I was saying, one of the participants in the group was a gentleman in his early 50s and someone who very rarely spoke during our discussions. We all made an effort to reach out to him in group or in person during breaks or otherwise, just to find out why is he not ready to share his story with the group. He would always be very curt and very aloof to a certain extent, and even rude, at times in keeping us at a distance.

At one point, some other participant shared his problems with his father throughout his childhood and how that impacted him and how he found it difficult to reach out to his father and how this created a lot of stress for him. While sharing, we found the gentleman sobbing very badly. He went to this young guy, who was sharing about the issues with his father, and said that it was not the lack of love that the boy's father was being so strict with him, but rather that it was for his well-being. He said, "Your father believes that by being stern with you, by being the disciplinarian in your life, he is ensuring that you turn out well and be a good human being and do well in your life."

Then he looked at the group and said, "I lost my son when he was 10 and it has been almost 15 years since. But I have not come out of the sorrow till date. I want to be strong for the sake of my other children that I don't want any weakness in me at any point in time. The reason I could not share my issue was that I felt that my problems were my weaknesses. By sharing, I am allowing myself that weakness. My biggest fear in this world is the safety of my children. I believe that if I am weak I can't take care of them."

We all have some demon or the other inside us. It could be a matter of the safety of children, of financial security, of acceptance in a relationship, of the fear of diseases or anything. As a part of our earlier journey, we have already discussed how crucial our fears are. They really drive our lives. They are behind some very strong behaviour of ours. You have already acknowledged the fears which are driving your life.

What is the deepest fear that makes you sick all the time? Take a moment and find out what causes a sinking feeling in your gut every time you think about it? What causes that enormous amount of fear inside you every time you worry about it? Please write down your answer here.

WHICH WAS THE HAPPIEST DAY OF YOUR LIFE?

We are now going to do a simple exercise.

Please follow my instructions clearly.

Which was the last movie you saw? Please remember it. If you sit quietly, shut your eyes and try playing the entire movie in your mind, what would happen? Let us see. So you are shutting your eyes and trying to remember the titles, the background at the time of the titles, the names of the actors or actresses, the director, the name of the movie and then the first scene of the movie. What was the background of that scene? How does it start? Is it with a close shot of a particular person or does it start with some kind of a backdrop may be a scene of a bustling town? What was the first dialogue of that movie?

Can you do this? Did you remember the movie? How far can you go like this? Trying to remember a particular situation you were in and trying to relive it is one of the greatest teaching tools for getting closer to yourself. I personally use it very often.

We could extend this tool further with another very powerful tool, which is used for meditation and self-exploration. This tool is called "Visualisation." Visualisation means trying to create an entire situation in front of your eyes by imagining every detail of it. It is very widely used in many training sessions, meditations and corporate sessions.

Let's start with a simple visualisation exercise as an example.

Imagine as if you have travelled to a hill station like Manali or Switzerland. Imagine you have got up very early like say at 5:00 AM. You feel fresh so you decide to take a nice walk in the early hours. You start your walk, you get out of the resort or hotel you are staying at and then you start walking on the road outside. You walk and walk and walk and walk some more. The morning is quite chilly… this lovely chill of early morning makes you cold. You shiver. You keep walking. You can smell the wild flowers and trees. You can feel the moist ground and the dampness of morning dew. Suddenly, you see a beautiful spot. Your road is leading to a beautiful opening of the valley. You can see mountains at the horizon and between you and the mountains is a beautiful valley. Just on the edge of the road, you see an amazingly solid rock so you decide to sit on it. You can feel the hard rock beneath you. You can also feel the wind or the morning breeze. You just look at the morning. You can see the slowly rising sun and as the sun rises you feel the warmth of the first sun rays on your face. You can see and hear birds chirping and flying here and there. Suddenly, the entire energy of the universe is entering into you. You rub your palms against each other and then massage your face with their warmth.

One of the most important factors of visualisation is to go into as much detail as possible. While trying to create these details, we get closer and closer to the situation we're trying to visualise. I personally love the power of visualisation because it helps me to live the moment of my choice.

Next few sections of this journey would require you to use this visualisation tool.

Before you arrive at what and how you need to change in your life, you need to figure out what impact I'm trying to create. And for that you need to be able to visualise some of the important factors of your life.

At this moment ask yourself to recollect the happiest day of your life so far. Was it the day you got married? Or was it the day you got your first job? Or was it the day you actually achieved something? Was it the day you met your friends and spent an entire day with them? It could be anything but you need to figure out which was the happiest day of your life so far. If you are struggling to find the happiest day maybe you can go with one of the happy days of your life.

Once you decided on which the happiest day of your life was, you need to actually recollect it with its every detail. Who were you with? What were you doing? What were the others doing? What were you wearing? What kind of emotions were you feeling? Was the happiness overwhelming? Was your happiness bringing tears to your eyes? Was anybody else as emotional as you on that day? Take a moment to remember it and replay, in details in your mind.

You need to be in comfortable surroundings with some solitude to be able to do this properly. Once you replay it with all possible details in your mind, please take a moment to write down some of those details here.

The happiest day of my life holds a secret towards the happiness in my life in general.

If you need to continue with the happy feeling which you felt on the happiest day in your life, what would you need to do? Who are the people you need to be with to feel that happy again? What would you be doing, in order to be happy like that? Answering these questions will require a lot of visualisation and a very strong self dialogue.

HOW DO YOU LOOK INTO THE FUTURE?

Please make yourself very comfortable first. Switch off your phone and other technical gizmos around you. Ensure that there are no pressing engagements or no place where you have to be. You need a solid hour or two, totally free, for yourself and the self dialogue.

Sit comfortably and try and understand the answer you gave about the happiest day of your life. What were you doing on that day? What was it about? Was it about your family? Was it about achievement? Was it about love? If you need to continue with that happy feeling, where do you need to focus in your life?

Let's imagine that you are 70 and you are being told that you have very few days left to live. Even though the end of your life is visible, the feeling you have is of total contentment, satisfaction and happiness. Satisfaction that you have lived a very fruitful and abundant life! You have achieved all that you wished for and you are there where you should be.

What would have you achieved? To reach that feeling of contentment and satisfaction and what would be the worth of your life? What would you have done? What goals would you have achieved? Who would be around you? What kind of house do you want to live in? Do you have a family? Who are there in your family? What are they doing?

At this stage, you need to take all the time and be very honest with yourself. You need to have a genuine self dialogue to understand what you want, to make you reach that state of contentment and fulfilling life. Take a moment and complete this exercise. Have as many details as possible. It will create as much depth as you want in this visualisation. Once you played this in your mind, you need to take a moment to write down some of the highlights here.

Now, if you need to have all those at the age of 70, use logic and understand what you need at the age of 50. By the time you become 50, what do you need to have so that you can have that fruitful and abundant feeling at 70? What would your career be like? What profession would you be in? What would you be doing? Where would you be staying? What would your family be like? Who all will be there? What would they be doing?

Take a moment to write your answers down. What would you have at 50 so that a path is paved for a blissful 70th year?

Let's be a little more playful and understand what it would take at the age of 40 for you to achieve what you want at the age of 50. What would you be doing at 40? Who would be around you when you are 40? Who would be close to you when you are 40? What profession would you pursue, when you are 40?

Let me make it a little more interesting and stretch it a little further. What would you need to do in the next five years so that all the things you have written above look feasible? What profession do you need to be in, in the next five years? What kind of money do you need to earn in the next five years? Who are the people you need to be with, in the next five years?

CHOOSE TO NURTURE

At this stage, you need to go back and read all the answers you have written down so far. Do you see any links with whatever you like and what you dislike and what you actually want for a fulfilling life? Do you see a connection in people you trust and people around you when you were at your happiest? Do you see a connection in your energy pattern and what makes you sick? Do you see a connection in your fears and the social situation around you? These connections will prove that all of it is linked! Everything is linked with every other thing. For our convenience, we look at it separately.

The answers you gave in this section represent things you want for a happy life, things which are absolutely crucial for you to build a life and fulfilling life ahead! You need to focus on them. You need to nurture them and protect them! You need find a way to work on these factors. You need to use various tools to increase their impact on your life. We are going to look at some simple tools and methods to facilitate this in the last section. But till then, the golden question is, what can you do now to make all the above things possible?

Take a moment to list the three things that you could change right now to create possibilities of the most fulfilling and abundant life for yourself.

____

____

____

____

HOW COMMITTED ARE YOU ON THIS JOURNEY?

How has been the journey so far? What are your feelings at this stage? What questions are coming to mind? How is your energy? What thoughts are on your mind? Are there any reservations? Please take a moment to note down these answers.

PART 3

Try it out

UNCLUTTERING YOUR SPACE!

We have entered a beautiful place in this journey where most of the questioning is done and now is the time to look for a few answers. We are going to explore and experience the power of small acts. This section will create huge possibilities of future just by doing some simple small things. Let's try.

At this stage, I want you to take this entire week and work with a simple agenda. The agenda is "un-cluttering!"

Could you start with physical un-cluttering? In your house, you may have your own room or maybe just a cupboard or you may have an entire house for yourself. At this stage you are going to target it and say, "Let me un-clutter my space, my physical space!" You are going to look at the attics, the lofts, the locked compartments of the cupboard and the cupboards as a whole, under the bed, over the cupboards, in the store room. In short, everywhere!

Go through everything, take things out and categorise them in what you use, what you need, what you don't use, what you don't need and stack them very carefully. What you keep is only what you need. What you don't need or what you don't use is something which you want to give away to those who may need it. This applies practically to everything: clothes, toys, gadgets, appliances, crockery, stationary, accessories and everything else. You are going to take a careful look at what you have stored and unnecessarily cluttered around yourself.

You want to scrutinise everything mercilessly and really keep what you need and what you use. The unnecessary clutter will have to be piled away first and then given away for sure. You are not allowed to keep it in any storeroom or in some shady corner of the house. No. You just will give it away and move it out of your life!

The next in line is your virtual space. You are going to look at your computer your phone, and then un-clutter it. If your computer has too many things on your desktop display you are going to remove them. Clear them from the desktop display and only keep those which you need on your desktop display. You are then going to look at your data. Is it scattered everywhere? Please file it into proper folders and create a logical storage for your data. The unnecessary one goes to recycle bin.

Then you are going to look at your mailbox. How many unread emails do you carry? How many mails are there in your inbox? Can you un-clutter here? Can you apply some rules to store away your mails in proper folders? Can you file them away in logical sequence in right folders? Are they too much? Do you feel you don't have enough time to un-clutter them right now? A simple idea- at this moment, create a folder of today's date and just move all the mails from your inbox in that folder. This way you will have a clean inbox and you also do not lose any correspondence for future reference. But then create the necessary rules and folders to pile away your incoming mails.

Now let's target your phone. Check all your contacts, delete those you don't need. Can you just remove them? Can you store those you need properly and can you ensure that all the necessary information is stored well? Can you do the same to your data on the phone? Can you please all the SMSs and all the photos and videos etc. Can you also ensured that all the necessary reminders for important days or important events or to do tasks are updated, logically sequenced and piled properly on your phone? Can you ensure that all the unnecessary applications and all the unnecessary clutter is removed immediately from you phone?

Now can you look at your bags, your wallet? Can you ensure that you un-clutter them completely can you ensure that they do not carry unnecessary bank statements, unnecessary bills or any other kind of garbage? Can you ensure that they are absolutely clean and clutter free?

Please do not hurry into this exercise. It may take a while; it may even take like a few days to two weeks. You are not in a hurry. You just need to set a target and ensure that you complete this exercise to the core. You remove all the clutter from everything around you. You don't want to pressurise yourself with unnecessary tight deadline to do this but at the same time you don't want to leave it open ended. So taking a realistic judgement set a target and then ensure that before the targeted date you have all the clutter in your life totally removed.

The physical space will have a major impact on your mind! Un-cluttering all the unnecessary garbage leaves you with only one more space with clutter. That's your mind! If you do the above mentioned un-cluttering really well, you will see it having a direct impact on your mind! Your mind will stop entertaining unnecessary feelings, any negativity, or any frustration! You will observe this change immediately.

Now that all the clutter in your life is gone how you do feel? Do you feel lighter? Do you feel anything is possible?

Do you feel ready to take on anything in this world? Do you fecl ready for the new possibilities? Do you feel your life now has a place for new possibilities? Take a moment and try to note down what did this experience of un-cluttering meant to you. Now that you have completed it successfully how does it make you feel?

YOUR SIGNALS FOR THE UNIVERSE

So many scholars have always spoken about energy which rules this universe. It has always intrigued me that we talk about so many frequencies and energies which are floating around and which get transferred from one person to another person, the vibes which all share and so on and so forth. I know many of you will find this concept difficult to digest. Let's assume that there is a kind of radio frequency which operates in this universe and each of us as a part of the universe is tuned with this particular frequency.

What kind of signals do you think are getting transferred from person to person? For example, let's say a lazy person who wakes up at 2:00 PM and probably sleeps for 18 hours a day or is too lazy to take a bath every day or too lazy to dress up and go to mingle with people, what kind of a signal is this person sending through this radio frequency? Any guesses? The way I read this signal is that the person is trying to say that he is too tired to try out anything new or maybe he's saying that he has just had enough action in his life or maybe he's saying that he is just not ready for any action. As he is tired the universe returns him with no action, no excitement, and no fun! If this person keeps wondering why nothing ever changes in life and how his life is so dull, where do you think it has gone wrong?

Let's take one more example. There is a person, perhaps in the late 30s or early 40s who has never been in any relationship.

That person is constantly sad. Now in sadness, what kind of signals is this person sending out? "I'm too sad and not ready for any kind of happy thing, I'm too sad to appreciate anything beautiful and happy around me!" or maybe, something like, "I'm just not ready to be happy." But on the other hand, in reality this person is actually wondering why he is not finding that one person who will bring him happiness!

Before some of you reach a judgement that what I'm saying is too far-fetched please hear me out completely. Before we take a decision that all this radio frequency and energies flowing in the universe is all a nonsensical talk, please bear with me a little more.

What kind of signals are you sending to the world? There is a huge possibility that the signals which you are sending are creating impressions which you may have not wanted to create, originally. Let's take one example. Are you too angry? What kind of a signal would an angry person send out? That everything in the world is wrong and all the wrong happens to me. Is it the impression you want to create?

Are you too selfish? What would a selfish signal mean? It seems that only you can take care of yourself nobody else thinks well about you, you need to constantly protect yourself because everyone is there to harm me. Is this real?

The most peculiar thing to think of here is whether you believe in the radio frequency not, whether you believe in the energy of the universe or not, the reality is that you actions are constantly sending out few signals to other people. You may want to call them impressions. Please accept that other people are going to react based only on those impressions. Sometimes, your actions and what you actually want to convey may not be aligned. That may be the reason for some gaps in what you receive!

At this stage please ask yourself what are the three most critical impressions you want to create and convey to everybody around you. These could be relevant for personal as well as professional life. Can you take a moment to write down what these three impressions are?

Do you want to be perceived as intelligent? What do you need to do for it? You need to figure out the actions which will pass on the message of your intelligence. To be perceived as intelligent you need to know your subject very well. You need to be available to pass on the information and be willing to pass on your knowledge. The most important dialogue is, are you doing this? Are your actions aligned with the impression you want to create? Are they in line with the signals you want to send?

Let's take another example. You want to be perceived as a young, vibrant and beautiful person. You want to be perceived as someone who is ready for love and commitment; what should your actions be in order to pass on this signal? You need to be dressed in youthful colours and be active and vibrant through the day. You need to share your love and readiness to commitment before you demand it in return.

If this is making sense, please look at the three impressions which you desperately want to create and convey to everybody around you. Please take a very logical look at all of it and write down all the possible actions which will convey each of these impressions.

AFFIRMATIONS

All through our lives we are constantly reprimanded for what we have not done rather than complemented on what we have done. Sometimes it is by other people but most times it is by our own selves that the focus is built on what is not done. If we rather build a habit to focus on what we have done and what we want to do then we will be bringing a lot of positive force in our lives.

Affirmations are a powerful tool to make this happen. Affirmations are a way to assert something which is already true or it could also be a pre-dictate of a proposition. How affirmations work are by constantly reminding yourself through simple sentences of things which you want to achieve or you have already achieved.

Without going into too much about the technicalities of affirmations, I want to focus on how we can use them as a tool for our existing journey. Affirmations are ways in which we can actually direct our thoughts and energies into a positive outcome which we want to achieve and that's exactly how we would use them in this exercise.

If my existing struggle is about losing weight, my affirmation should be something as simple as, "I choose to exercise regularly." If my existing pursuit is of control over myself I need to say to myself something as simple as, "I am at peace." If I am trying to overcome my constant struggle between all my likes and dislikes, I need to say something as simple as, "I am grateful."

These are very beautiful affirmations which will help us in our chosen journey. One of the most beautiful assertions which has helped me is, "I know what I know."

We're stuck in our own struggle and its merits and demerits and its positives and negatives that we sometimes forget to look around us and admire the beauty of the journey. The constant pursuit of some or the other achievement which at times is hard to achieve, fills our life with unnecessary sorrow, frustration or negativity. In such situations, a simple affirmation like, "Everything I need comes to me at the perfect time" can clear the mind and set our energies in the right direction.

There are separate online courses available on how to use your affirmations for your own struggle. We are using affirmations as a part of this journey to create positivity around you. Affirmations should be used to sustain yourself belief and faith in your capabilities and competence. It is said that each should create his own affirmations so to make them most effective. If you do a simple internet search, you will find readymade lists of affirmations available for your use.

For this particular journey let's do a simple exercise and try to create our own affirmations. Please look at your biggest struggles, your biggest challenges and the biggest setbacks that you have mentioned in this book. Go through your previous answers and find out what you feel are the most challenging part or troublesome emotions of your life. Then create a simple affirmation around it. For example, if you think, "I'm low on self-confidence," your affirmation should be "I feel confident." If your struggle is of keeping your focus intact on a particular goal then you should say "I choose to focus on this goal."

Let me take a moment to write down at least five affirmations which will help me for the further journey.

Please choose an appropriate place to display your affirmations so that you can revisit them again and again throughout the day. You can choose to print them or write them and put it up on your workstation or on your refrigerator or you may just choose to make it your desktop background or your mobile phone background. Please go with what you think is right. The purpose is to ensure that you see them again and again and get to repeat it again and again. Please ensure that in the morning when you're looking at the mirror looking into your own eyes you say these affirmations out loud and clear to yourself. This is going to be of immense impact before you even realise. Please follow it as a ritual. Please note that affirmations said with a lot of emotion and passion will bring you a lot more benefit. Please remember for affirmations to show its impact, there are certain key characteristics which are crucial. They need to be clear. They need to be concise. They need to be said aloud every day. They need to be repeated multiple times of the day.

I am grateful for the journey so far.

YOUR IDEAL DAY

We are going to look at all your answers and build an ideal day for you. Let this just one day be exactly how it should be, ideally.

Please take a look at your energy patterns and figure out how you energy works. Decide how you want to divide your day as per that pattern. Please take your most energetic part of the day and put a task from what you absolutely enjoy, into your to-do list.

Take the person who puts a smile on your face and plan a full hour with that person. Go out to some interesting place or stay at home. Do something creative with that person. Please plan it ahead to ensure that that person is also free.

Take two things from what makes your life happy and see what you can do to create those two things on this day, or what can you do enjoy these things on this day. Please plan them in the slot where your energy is comparatively high.

Set an hour aside to calling up, meeting those people who trust completely. Have a generic chat with them. If possible, meet them and have a cup of coffee with them. Please plan this ahead.

Take an hour to plan and learn a new skill. In the coming six months, promise yourself that you will learn something new. Find out more about it. Check all your possible options and take steps to start learning that skills from this ideal day of yours.

Once you plan this day, plan to live one day as per this schedule. Just one day. Not more. Not every day but just one day!

After you spend one day as per the plan, take a moment to write down what possibilities you see in the future. How can you spend more time in a better way? Please write down three changes you can make to your life in order to ensure that you have enough time to do things which matter the most to you.

TAMING THE FEAR

As we have already discussed that all fear that we have is a result of a certain belief we have. That belief will give rise to some peculiar behaviour of ours.

Your fear of safety for your family will make you overprotective. It will make you think of bad things first and then get worried all the time. This is coming out of the belief that you can protect you family.

What if we change the belief that forms the basis of our fear? What if you stop believing that you can protect your family? Can you really protect your family? The answer is no. The reality is we can only learn to be cautious and that's what I can also teach my family. To be more cautious! Your belief should be that you can teach your family to be more cautious. Now check what happens to your fear. Suddenly, your fear will start looking blurred and you will opportunities to deal with that fear.

Please go to the page where you spoke about what makes you sick all the time in your gut. Check that and ask what belief is driving that sinking feeling. Follow this process. Ask what your actions because of this fear are. List those actions. Now ask that you do all this successfully what will happen? That will lead you to the belief you have behind this fear. There could be multiple beliefs resulting into a single fear.

List all these beliefs. Now ask yourself how you can change these beliefs. What happens if you remove the compulsion to act on these beliefs? What happens if you allow yourself

FUN RELATIONSHIP SCALE

Communication	Reacting to issues	Decision making	Fights / Conflicts	Expectations
Alternative behaviour patterns				
Fruitful communication/ Things are discussed objectively/ Lot of genuine appreciation. Facts based / Genuine listening	Acceptance and objectivity-Okay so we do have these issues. / I can do this… To solve these issues. / We can get on top of this…/ Win -win approach / readiness to listen to the other point of view	Discuss and Decide-Let's discuss what can be done here. / I respect your opinion / Hey… You make a lot of sense /	Issue-based fighting-Well this is going wrong / We need to solve it together / Let me protect my interest but not on your expense. / I know you were right about this / Sorry… It won't happen again	Understood and accepted expectations-Okay so we know what we want / I love you so I will do it / Hey listen… I don't want to do it right now but maybe later / Hey do you mind but I don't want to do it / I am ok with what you have decided
Opinion based communication / Very less or forced appreciation / lot of finger pointing. / limited listening	Arguments / Very obsessive outlook towards the issue / Everything is an issue-mostly life changing / only one person taking blame all the time	Clear division of areas / Lets not step into each other's areas / I don't agree that this is the best decision but I will go with it. / acceptance with reluctance	I am tired of fighting / Lets do something different so that we won't fight / You are wrong / I am to be blamed. / Sorry… At least that should stop the fight now…	I want you to do this… / Do it for me darling / Please… Please / Well I know what will make you do this / Can't we just discuss what we expect from each other

Increasing level of maturity ↑

Communication compulsion-Everything has to be discussed / Everything has to be said / lack of listening / one person communicating	Issue? Where is the issue? I don't see any issues / Things are just getting out of hands / I have been trying so much but nothing is good enough / avoiding issues / no one accepting defeat /	Let's have it your way / Ok how does it matter? Finally you will do what you want / If I stay out of this we won't fight. / I have to take all the decisions all the time/ You don't take any responsibility.	Let's discuss this later / Can we stop talking about it? / I refuse to let go / You make me miserable / This is your problem / This is it! I can't take this anymore / I don't know why I am taking this shit…	My god… You expect so much / Whatever I do is not enough so let me just not do it / I don't know what to expect from you. / I don't what do I want /
No communication/ Answer only when asked / Avoid talking	Let's discuss it right now. / Very emotional / Very superficial reaction	I don't care / I know the best	Yelling / Insisting on fighting / Refusing to fight or even talk	Oh god… I did not expect this… / You never do what I want / Do you even know what I want?
Communication	Reacting to issues	Decision Making	Fights / Conflicts	Expectations

to believe that you have an ability to impact all these beliefs? What actions can you take to do so? Please list those actions here.

Please note that at any given time certain aspects of your life would be out of your control. But that should not result into an uncontrollable fear. Some fears are good. They motivate us to do the right things and put our side of efforts. But they should not drive our lives. We should encourage beliefs which will pamper such fears!

REVIVING RELATIONS

One of the most important aspects which will help us for a beautiful journey in life is the healthy relationships we create around us. Please take a moment and look through your answers on the people you want to be with among the people around you, the people you dislike and the person who makes you happy, the person who brings a smile to your face. Please go through all your previous answers around relationships and people around you and identify a single relationship which will have an immense impact on your immediate future.

We have, in our first section, discussed the importance of a relationship, and that is trust. Please select a relationship which will have immense impact, but at the same time, at this stage it is not at your desired level of trust and comfort. What we're going to do is that we could use an interesting scale to look at the various aspects of a relationship, taking help of the examples chosen and then figuring out how to plot our relationships on various parameters and then figuring out a way to take that relationship to the next level.

On the subsequent page, I'm presenting you something which is called "Fun Relationships Scale." Please understand that this is just a tool which is a representative way of identifying where your relationships stand and how can you take them to the next level. Please use it in the same spirit. The scale presented below has various aspects which are important in a relationship and levels at which you react in each of those aspects considering the maturity of your relationship. It would be interesting to sit with someone and discuss this if you are plotting a particular relationship on this key. If you can do it with the same person it would have immense benefit in it. However if you are not comfortable, you doing it on your own is also worth a try.

After you plot your relationship on various aspects please try and look at the certain indicators provided in the next level of this relationship scale. What would it take for you to perform as per the indicators provided in the next level? Please take a moment to identify the actions you would take, to take a certain relationship in your life to next level.

Based on your current behaviour pattern you can see where your relationship stands on 5 key areas mentioned here. These behaviours are representatives of the maturity level of the relationship. Please check where you stand on those and then see how that relationship looks. What can be done to improve that? For this answer please look at the next box to understand how can you change your actions. This will help you to derive a new meaning out of this relationship. Whenever you are comfortable you can try and do this exercise with the concerned person as well.

EMOTIONS

I'm now going to enter into a space called emotions. Unfortunately, it is one of the most widely abused words. Because of the abuse and references made to it in the wrong places it has developed a connotation of being very mushy or somehow, relates to hypersensitivity. To make things simpler right in the beginning, let's understand that there is a difference between emotions and being emotional. Though there is nothing wrong in being emotional, for the sake of this discussion I'm going to state right in the beginning that we are discussing emotions here and there is nothing emotional about it.

Most of us in most situations spend a lot of energy in denying or defending a particular emotion. Let me give you an example. If somebody has done something to hurt you and you are feeling angry with that person, half the struggle is about feeling so angry that you are so angry. How can you feel so angry? Why am I feeling so angry? The moment we start asking these questions the answer is going to be why you should not feel so angry or how feeling so angry is wrong. This answer could come from somebody else or it could be our own. The struggle becomes about defending the anger. However, if we just replace this entire fight with a simple sentence like 'I am feeling angry', what would happen then? Now the reaction would be why you are feeling so angry so the focus gets shifted on the issue rather than you as a person.

You can use the same logic for any emotion you may be defending. For example if you have just had a breakup but you are still feeling very sad and you miss your ex, rather than constantly saying, "Why on earth am I missing my ex all the time?" or "How can I miss him or her so much?" and then spending all of your energy in justifying how your ex was a bad person, what if you just accept that you miss him or her? The discussion could go on to discuss about some of the happy moments you've had in your relationship and some of the traits or characteristics of your ex which make you miss him or her a lot. However, this would be a far better conversation rather than just trying to say that nothing in your relationship was right and despite that, you miss your ex so much.

One of the most important aspects of a happy and cheerful life is to have tremendous amount of comfort with the emotions we feel. Let's say it aloud-anger is one of the most authentic emotions. It's only when it gets converted into revenge or deceit that it becomes a dangerous tool. But as an emotion, anger is one of the most authentic and beautiful emotions because it says 'I care'. Think about it. When you genuinely get angry with somebody you actually are operating from the position of care. Till the time you are operating out of a position of care, your emotion has to be beautiful. The moment you allow yourself this particular space, your struggle is going to be about conveying your care in the right way to the other person rather than just spending energy thinking about how angry you are.

In a similar way, love is a very beautiful and authentic emotion. It's only when it gets converted into lust or selfishness that it starts becoming dangerous. Love operates from a position of respect and if there is respect, how can it be bad?

In this way, we can go on discussing all the emotions possible in the human world. Please understand that by giving yourself the freedom to feel a particular emotion, you're actually going to reduce the risk of them getting converted into something dangerous.

Take a moment to note down certain emotions that you feel uncomfortable about. Let's choose three emotions that you want to feel. You should be creating space around yourself to feel them. Let's identify various ways in which you can create that space.

YOU AND YOUR WORLD

Congratulations! We are at the last stop on this beautiful journey. This is where we create a beautiful picture of our desired future. Please take a moment to go through all the answers you have written down so far in this journey. Do take a break if you still want to say something to yourself. If you have read so far, you've done very well.

Now as a last exercise, we are going to do something to bring a lot of fun and a lot of happiness in your life. That is why it is important to ensure that you have no dialogue pending, and that there are no half-hearted answers remaining.

We are now going to create a beautiful collage of your life. This collage will be called, "Me and my world!" To make it simpler and easier, let's divide our life into four parts. The four parts of this world are going to be "Values" you operate with, live for and respect. "Dreams" which you have to achieve or conquer. "Passions" which are important to you, which make you happy and which always bring a lot of joy to you and finally, "Beliefs" which fill your life, which guide you through difficult situations and which are sacred to you.

Now, on a piece of paper, please mark out four parts and write all the four titles on top of each part. One by one, think deeply and figure out what these four words mean to you and in your life and world. What are the values which are important to you? What are the dreams you have? What passions do you carry? What are the beliefs you really believe in? Take as much time as required to work on this. At this stage, we are not creating anything beyond just a list of words which will remind us of what we want in these four categories. At this stage, it is an individual exercise. It will require a lot of solitude, thinking, self dialogue, and references to the previous answers you have written down. Take as much time as you need and make the list robust. Any word that comes to your mind, any sentence that comes to your mind, please go on writing them down under the relevant section.

There will come a stage which will create so much happiness around you. Choose a weekend that is totally free. There should be no official, personal, professional and social engagements pending. It has to be an absolutely free weekend, two full days at your disposal. Bring in a lot of old magazines, colourful papers, colourful pens, glue and a huge sheet of white paper. Refer to the list you have created above. On this big sheet of paper, create a collage which will represent the four areas of your life according to the list you have already created. I'm going to share an example with you just for the sake of clarity. However, use them just for the sake of a reference. The fun would be to create your own collage.

Once you create a collage, once you've done your basic work, I would encourage you to bring in people who are very important for your future. It could be your family, it could be your friends, and, to a certain extent, it could be even your bosses or your colleagues. Share this collage with them. If it is comfortable, take their inputs. If possible, involve them in another collage-making activity and try and build a collage as a group. Do whatever is necessary to make it as realistic as possible. Use cut outs from magazines pictures, words, phrases, colours. Make it so attractive that anybody should feel like looking at it and most importantly you should feel like looking at it. It should inspire you!

Example:

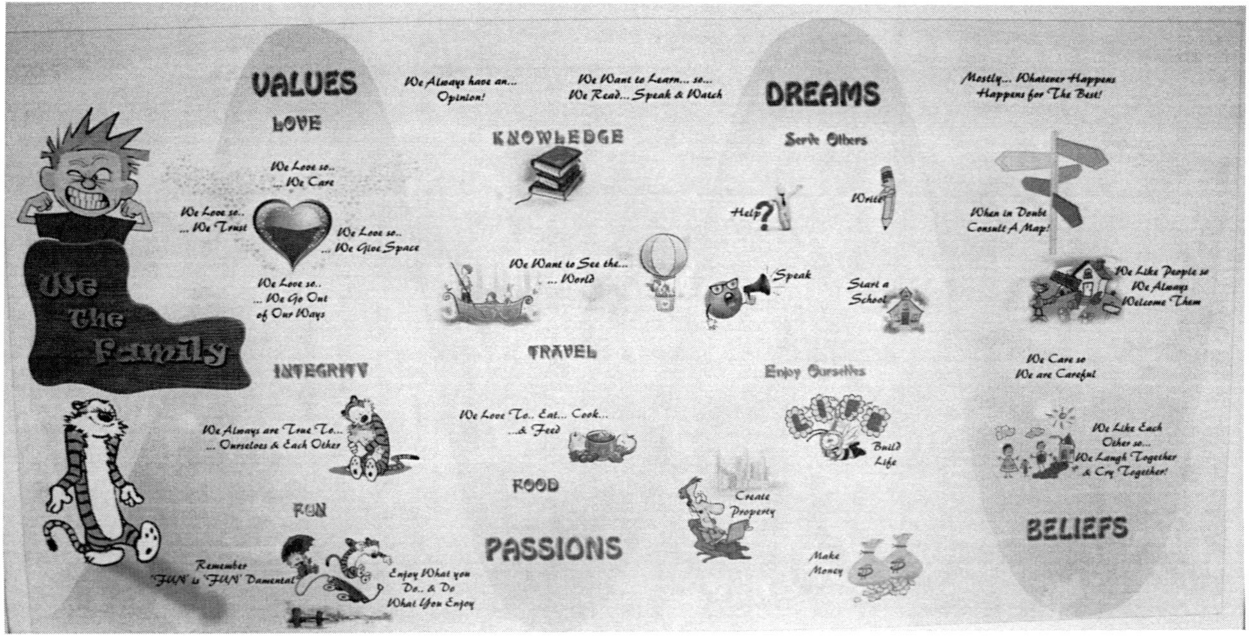
VALUES
LOVE
We Love so..
... We Trust
We Love so..
... We Care
We Love so..
... We Give Space
We Love so..
... We Go Out
of Our Ways
We The Family
INTEGRITY
We Always are True To...
... Ourselves & Each Other
FUN
Remember
'FUN' is 'FUN' Damental
Enjoy What you
Do.. & Do
What You Enjoy
We Always have an...
Opinion!
We Want to Learn... so...
We Read... Speak & Watch
KNOWLEDGE
We Want to See the...
... World
TRAVEL
We Love To.. Eat... Cook...
...& Feed
FOOD
PASSIONS
DREAMS
Serve Others
Help
Write
Speak
Start a
School
Enjoy Ourselves
Build
Life
Create
Property
Make
Money
Mostly... Whatever Happens
Happens for The Best!
When in Doubt
Consult A Map!
We Like People so
We Always
Welcome Them
We Care so
We are Careful
We Like Each
Other so...
We Laugh Together
& Cry Together!
BELIEFS

Congratulations! You have successfully completed this journey. However, as you would realise, this is just the beginning of something far more beautiful and wonderful. Your life ahead!

I hope you are feeling as energised as I am. If you feel even a little closer to yourself, I would say that my purpose is achieved!

In the end, I want to conclude by saying that happiness is energy. Like any physical energy, it would be created only with movement or motion. The more active you stay in life, the more you do things, and happiness will be attracted to your life.

I want to end this soulful journey with three simple affirmations-

I am happy!

I am loved!

I have what I need!